Managing Change in Life: Elijah's Strategy

– BENJAMIN ACEHAMPONG MBA –

An environmentally friendly book printed and bound in England by
www.printondemand-worldwide.com

http://www.fast-print.net/bookshop

MANAGING CHANGE IN LIFE

A catalogue record for this book is available from the British Library

ISBN 978-178456-268-7

First published 2016 by
FASTPRINT PUBLISHING
Peterborough, England.

TABLE OF CONTENTS

DEDICATION

To my beloved parents of blessed memories Opanyin William Mantey Acheampong and Madam Elizabeth Adwoa Owiredua for the culture of respect and integrity they instilled in me.

To my beloved wife Lady Regina Acheampong who has stood beside me through thick and thin, my two sons Ethniel and Othniel Acheampong, with a hope that the content and principles in this book will guide and become the quality of your character in waiting on God for His direction any time you are to make a decision based on changes in your condition.

ACKNOWLEDGEMENTS

'Let everything that hath breath praise the Lord. Praise ye the Lord'. Psalm 150:6. All my thanks and appreciation and honour goes to God who gave me life and inspiration in doing what I love doing. THANK YOU.

There are many people I would like to thank for their encouragement and support to this work. I am forever grateful to everyone who saw the greatness in me when I couldn't see it and sometimes doubted my capabilities but they kept on pushing me to the limit.

Without them this book would not have been possible and published for everyone to read. I am honoured to have people like Anthea Attram, Dr. Shaminder Takhar, Rev & Mrs Ofori Temeng (ICGC, Nsawam), Angela Owusu Ansah, Mrs Michelle Acquah, Rev Emmanuel Ekow Amoah, Samuel S. Acheampong, Kukua Neizer, Angela Nikoi, Francis Konadu and spiritual sons and daughters and the entire Greater Works Chapel International family.

Thank you all.

INTRODUCTION

Change is inevitable and, whether you are a believer or not a believer, it is something you cannot just avoid. Our Father is a progressive and dynamic Father. He is one that expects His children to grow in every area of their lives. This type of growth comes in stages and each stage brings a change. **1 Peter 2:2 'As new born babes, desire the pure milk of the word, which you may grow thereby'**. Stagnation is an abomination to our father who is in Heaven. He has set things in motion since creation. In the below scriptures we see the nature of the Father in motion:

Ecclesiastics3:1 ***'To everything there is a season, a time for every purpose under Heaven's.*** What this scripture is saying is that nothing happen by chance. God has pre-ordained in the life of the believer what must happen. We only need to ask Him to show us His will concerning our earthly living.

> ***'Because the people who are crazy enough to think they can change the world, are the ones who do.'***
>
> ***Apple Inc.***

Anything that has a beginning has an end.

Dan 2:21 ***'And he changeth the times and the seasons: he removeth kings, and setteth up kings: he***

giveth wisdom unto the wise, and knowledge to them that know understanding':

Wow, listen to what this scripture in Daniel is saying, He (God) changes the times and seasons. It means that there are no changes in our lives, favourable or adverse, that are the work of the devil. Some of them are caused by God. I believe the ones that are caused by God are to make us grow or mature spiritually in God. The causes that are not caused by God are caused by satan through our own choices.

1 Thessalonians 5:1 'But concerning the times and the seasons, brethren, you have no need that I should write to you'.

He makes things beautiful in its time. My dear friend please understand me on this point that between the time of the prophecy and the time of its fulfilment is a waiting period.

What do you do when change happens? Is there a possibility that we can see change coming? How do we survive when there is a sudden change in our lives? These are some of the questions that we will be looking to answer. Managing your life as a Christian in this uncertain world is very important and crucial to our spiritual and physical well-being.

Many Christians muddle through life when there is a sudden change in their circumstances, for example when a brother or sister travels abroad or to an environment he or she is not familiar with . Working with someone who does not believe in your faith can be a dramatic change in your spiritual life. Now, how do you survive that change? The Bible declares, 'We are in this world but we are not from this world' (John 17:14). In fact, it goes ahead to declare that we are pilgrims or sojourners. You see, it is crucial in this very moment that something must be done about what we are seeing today.

Many things cause individuals, corporate bodies or Churches to grow through change, for example, growth (childhood, adolescent, adulthood), economic downturn or tragic circumstance, to mention just a few. In this context, one has to be able to introduce and manage that kind of sudden change until their situation gradually becomes better.

The Bible is full of people and nations that went through series of changes of some sort and in all cases these people or nations adopted Godly strategies to survive that kind of change in their circumstance. It also contains stories of people whose lives were turned around by some of the changes they went through by the help of the almighty God.

However, let me introduce you to some of the changes that can occur in our lives. Losing a job in economic meltdown is followed by questions such as: how do you pay for your mortgage, school fees of your children, fuel the vehicle, put food on the table, clothe those little kids and take the family on holidays?

Losing a loved one: husband, wife, father, mother, sibling, son or daughter. How do you replace them? You have to live with it forever. If you were being sponsored in a college or university and that kind of support ceased all of a sudden, how do you continue your education?

Now, let us assume that you were able to finish college or university and three years later you still haven't been able to find a job. Your parents are fed up of you staying at home; how do you cope with the situation OR survive that change?

Let's say you have been married for twelve years and you are waiting for the fruit of the womb. How do you survive the external pressures from parents who are desperate for their grandchildren?

You start a business and invite a good friend, more importantly a Christian brother or sister to assist so both of you could do it together. He or she later approaches you with the idea that he or she wants to take over the business or even ditch you in the process. You disagree with that idea. The next moment he or she stabs you in the back and starts his or her own, which is not a problem, but takes everything both of you bought. How do you survive such a dramatic change?

These are not just formulated stories, they are real-life scenarios.

You have been married to your wife or husband for some years now with kids. One decides to quit the marriage for reasons best known to him or her. How do you survive this kind of change?

A young, energetic and vibrant lady or man has an accident and loses a leg or arm. How do they survive this change?

I call all these **'LEAN SEASONS'** because nothing happens during these lean seasons. At the moment, life becomes stressful and full of thoughts.

In the light of the above we will be looking at why these changes happen from a biblical perspective. We will look at whether they are ordained by God or just demonic as it's been perceived that every change that occurs in our lives which is considered to be 'bad' is the work of the devil. You will be introduced to some of the strategies adopted by biblical characters which enabled them to survive change. We must bear in mind that although we can learn from the universities of our world, we also learn by our life experiences and how we master these experiences makes us masters in life situations. This is what I call **'The Disciplines of Life'**.

CHAPTER 1
Defining Change

As it's been defined, change is an act or process through which something becomes different. Change defines all building blocks required to bring about a given long-term goal, whether on an individual level or organisational level. This set of interchangeable connected building blocks is referred to as an outcomes, result, accomplishment or precondition.

A theory of change describes the types of interventions that bring about positive outcomes. Each outcome in the pathway of change is tied to an intervention, revealing the often complex web of activity that is required to bring about change.

Change is a specific and measurable description of a social change initiative that forms the basis for strategic planning, on-going decision-making and evaluation. The methodology used to create change is also usually referred to as a process or result.

Any good planning and evaluation method for change requires individuals or organisation to be clear on long-term goals, identify measurable indicators of success and formulate actions to achieve goals.

It differs from any other method of describing initiatives in a few ways:

- It shows a causal pathway from here to there by specifying what is needed for goals to be achieved.
- It requires you to articulate underlying assumptions which can be tested and measured.
- It changes the way of thinking about initiatives from what you are doing to what you want to achieve and starts there.

Change provides a road map or a compass to get you from one place to a destination. If it is good and complete, your road map can be read by others and show that you know how to chart your course.

More importantly, if it is good and complete, you have the best chance of making the change in the world you set out to make and of demonstrating your successes and your lessons along the way.

The Purpose of Change

Why change? Is it at all necessary to make a change in situations and circumstances? On what conditions and basis will one make a change? What kind of impact will this kind of change bring? What are the benefits of change? These are all questions that may come into the mind of an individual or organisation that wants to create change. Sometimes change just happens.

Any business in today's fast-moving environment that is looking for the pace of change to slow is likely to be sorely disappointed. In fact, businesses and individuals should embrace change. Change is important for any organisation or individual because, without change, businesses would be likely to lose their competitive edge and fail to meet the needs of what their customers want.

Without change, business leaders still would be dictating correspondence to secretaries, editing their words and sending them back to the drawing board, wasting time for all involved. Change that results from the adoption of new technology is common in most organizations and while it can be disruptive at first, ultimately the change tends to increase productivity and service.

Technology also has affected how we communicate. No longer do business people dial a rotary phone, get a busy signal and try again and again and again until they get through. No longer do business people have to laboriously contact people, in person, to find out about other people who might be useful resources - they can search for experts online through search engines as well as through social media sites.

Today's burgeoning communication technology represents changes that allow organisations to learn more, more quickly, than ever before.

Customers who were satisfied with conventional ovens many years ago are sometimes impatient with the microwave today. As the world evolves, people need change and grow, creating new demand for new types of products and services - and opening up new areas of opportunity for companies to meet those needs.

Spiritual Perspective of Change

The world is a place or a stage for perpetual change. The Psalmist declared in his writings, 'The sun rises and sets, the moon waxes and wanes, the tide rises and falls. Seed-time and harvest, summer and winter, day and night will never pass away.'

Changes come alike to all, even the inevitable change to which Job refers, 'All the days of my appointed time will I wait, till my change come' **(Job 14:14).** Everyone experiences change at different times and stages of life.

The changes of which Job speaks are those changes we least expect: changes that disturb our arrangements, unhinge our plans, and frustrate our hopes; changes like earthquakes upheave all order, comfort and settled ease. Without such changes we are liable to drift into the perils of an undisturbed life and pleasant monotony breeds ignorance of God. When a man's life is filled with blessings and is never darkened by storms, there is the fear that the absence of change will rob him of deeper life in Christ.

Elijah was a man of many situations and conditions. He was much tried yet much favoured. The circumstances upon which our text would be taken from refer to the tragic era in his life when he found himself lonely and attacked by a king (King Ahab) who married an evil woman (Jezebel). But his trials drove him nearer to God. He knew only too well that uninterrupted prosperity was apt to cause neglect of higher things.

When a train of challenges attends us and we look at our afflictions, losses and crosses and cry out, 'All these changes are against me'! Let us take comfort in reading God's word,

'It is good for me that I have been afflicted' (Ps.119:71).

I have observed something else under the sun. The fastest runner doesn't always win the race, and the strongest warrior doesn't always win the battle. The wise sometimes go hungry, and the skilful are not necessarily wealthy. And those who are educated don't always lead successful lives. It is all decided by chance, by being in the right place at the right time. (Ecclesiastes 9:11)

I said in my prosperity, I will never be moved' (Ps. 30:6 NASB).

The prosperity of the placed life often produces self-confidence and forgetfulness of God. When the heart's desires are fulfilled and there is freedom from impoverishing changes, the need for God is not even small. Unbroken prosperity is spiritually dangerous. In whom does nothing but win and prosper seldom a chastened, spiritually refined, sympathetic person.

'Uninterrupted, monotonous success sometimes breeds atheism'.

The paradox of faith however, is that we are built up by being broken down. God does by undoing; He makes as He breaks. Reverse and change are tools for the shaping of character. Change is a phase of divine ministry. God takes us back to move us forward. The waves go out and return with fuller force.

Life changes always as it should and constantly awakens fear which lead us nearer to God. They are stepping stones for change.

Whatever changes that occur in our lives are for a good purpose and our perception of them matters a lot.

Causes of Change

Looking at your physical self is an indication that change has taken place: losing a job, losing a loved one, sudden change in national or personal economy, divorce, losing a body part - say, an eye - through an accident, banks possessing your house due to continual non-payment, graduating from university without a job. The list goes on but we must remember that these are all seasonal changes that people go through whether they are believers or non-believers. But do we stop living? The answer is a big NO. These seasonal changes; although they are being experienced as negative, they will change to become positive if we can persevere.

Galatians 6:9 'And let us not grow weary while doing good for in due season we shall reap if we do not lose heart'. The emphasis is on 'we do not lose heart'.

Spiritual Change

Persecution had compelled Paul the Apostle to leave Thessalonica, and in his letters he tells Christians there how they ought to live and to await the Lord's return with constant diligence. By so doing they will be sure of their rapture to meet the Father.

1Thessolonias 5:3 ***'And the very God of peace sanctify you wholly; and I pray God your whole spirit and soul and body be preserved blameless unto the coming of our Lord Jesus Christ'.***

> ***'Education is the most powerful weapon which you can use to change the world.'***
>
> ***– Nelson Mandela***
>
> 

We can see vividly from this scripture that man is tripartite, meaning man is made of soul and spirit which lives in a body. In other words Paul the Apostle encourages us to grow spiritually, physically and bodily. And in growing spiritually, changes will definitely take place. Remember, a false balance is an abomination to God. I argue that both three parts must be developed.

Let us look at this very scripture as well in Corinthians.

2Corinthians 5:17 ***'Therefore, if anyone is in Christ, he is a new creation; old things have passed away; behold, all things have become new'.***

My understanding of this very piece of scripture is no matter how old one may be - say, 75 years old - and you just gave your life to Jesus Christ and accepted Him as your Lord and personal saviour; spiritually, God sees you as a day-old baby. For that matter there is a need for you to grow. This growth will take place in stages and changes will start taking place right away. Now this is a fully grown physical person and spiritually he or she is a day old. How do you balance the equation? If you used to drink, smoke or chase after women, there has to be a constant effort of stopping such behaviour. Because this type of change in a person's life is difficult, many people do not want to go through with it. But the fact of the matter is that we cannot compromise on the word of God. It is either here or there. It cannot be in between.

What do we mean by spiritual change and growth? I know most of you might know or some would be wondering what this means. This was the exact question Nicodemus asked Jesus in ***John 3:1-4 'There was a man of the Pharisees named Nicodemus, a ruler of the Jews. This man came to Jesus by night and said to Him, 'Rabbi, we know (agree, accept, believe) that you are a teacher come from God; for no one can do these signs that You (Jesus) do unless God is with Him. (Acts 10:38). Jesus answered and said to him, 'Most assuredly, I say to you, unless one is born again, he cannot see the Kingdom of God. Nicodemus said to Him, 'How can a man be born when he is old? Can he enter a second time into his mother's womb and be born? Jesus answered, Most assuredly, I say to you, unless one is born of water and the spirit', he cannot enter the Kingdom of God'.***

This conversation Jesus had with Nicodemus explains or gives us a picture of what I was saying earlier on. Once you become born again and being just a day old (spiritually), you cannot straight away start chewing bones and eating solid foods. Typically this is about physical growth. Similarly to grow spiritually, you must change your way of thinking and start doing things such as attending Bible classes to learn about God through the teaching of His word; memorising scriptures, acting and living by faith daily, and through daily quiet time will ensure your spiritual growth.

Now what do we mean by being born of water and spirit? According to the Bible, baptism by immersion is a replica of His (Jesus') death and resurrection which makes us anew. Being born of the spirit also means receiving the fresh breath of God. When God created man from the dust of the earth, man was lying down according to Genesis and the breath of God came into man through his nostrils and man became a living soul.

In **Luke 3:16-17,** ***John the Baptist answered, saying to all, 'I indeed baptise you with water, but One mightier than I is coming, whose sandal strap I am not worthy to loosen. He (Jesus) will baptise you with the Holy Spirit and fire. His winnowing fan is in His hand, and He will thoroughly clean out His threshing floor, and will gather the wheat into His barn; but the chaff He will burn with unquenchable fire'.***

Dear brother and sister, being born of the spirit is very important to every Christian who wants to see a greater change and growth spiritually. This type of baptism can only be received by those washing by the water. Luke tried to portray the humility of John the Baptist. The baptism of the spirit was made possible after the death and resurrection of our Lord Jesus Christ which was spoken in the Acts of the Apostles. Acts 2:4. The fan used to blow the chaff away from the wheat will separate the chaff from the wheat, which is a violent process. The wheat alone is accepted and all that's not of God will be consigned to Hell.

As we grow spiritually, the way that we perceive the world should be changing for the better. For example, in the early stages of our spiritual development, we might take a relatively bad experience that we have and simply chalk it up to being bad luck, and possibly play a victim role in how events unfold. We react to the experience in a negative way and make little or no growth from it.

As we make spiritual growth, we can choose better actions to deal with such negative experiences, turning them into positive ones. Instead of playing a victim role when something bad happens, we can reflect and look for the deeper meaning, and try to see our part in how we might have brought such an event on.

As we grow spiritually, our attitude shifts for the better, in a number of ways. Spiritual growth isn't so much about changing our world or our lives, but about changing ourselves and how we perceive the world. It is like waking up and seeing the world through 'a new pair of glasses'.

One of the ways our attitude changes is in terms of pride and humility. As we make spiritual progress, pride starts to melt away as we realise that we really don't know it all, and that every experience can become a learning opportunity for us if we approach it with genuine humility. People that we might have dismissed in the past come to have new meaning for us because we know that each person might have a potential lesson to teach us. Pessimism doesn't play well with this idea. Instead, we start looking for the silver lining in things, in terms of our experiences and what we might possibly learn from them.

Our connections with others change as we grow spiritually. One way that this happens is mentioned above, in that we come to see others as potential teachers. Another way that our relationships change is that we tend to place more value on them as we grow, and there is also a tendency towards reaching out and helping others. These ideas replace what is normally selfish and self-seeking behaviour that used to dominate our lives.

A holistic approach to our life and our overall health comes into being, as we start to realise that everything relates to our spiritual growth. For example, we might start eating better, quit smoking or start exercising and so on. We see the connectness of these holistic ideas and realise that we cannot make further growth until we address certain problem areas. A balanced lifestyle becomes the goal, as we see how this further helps us to grow spiritually.

In addition to these ideas, spiritual growth is also characterised by a growing connection with a higher power, which some might experience through prayer and meditation. We come to learn that our greatest teacher can be either the stranger we meet on the corner, but also the quiet or still mind that we achieve in solitude while meditating on the most holy word of God which is the Bible.

Physical Change

Ecclesiastes 3: 2, A time to be born and a time to die; a time to plant, and a time to pluck what is planted.

Physical changes occur when a person undergoes a change that does not change their spiritual nature. A physical change involves a change in physical properties. Physical properties can be observed without changing the type of matter. Examples of physical properties include shape, size, colour, odour and weight. Consider the following:

> ***'Change will not come if we wait for some other person, or if we wait for some other time. We are the ones we've been waiting for. We are the change that we seek.'***
>
> ***– Barack Obama***
>
> 

An example of a physical change occurs when making a baseball bat. Wood is carefully crafted into a shape which will allow a batter to best apply force to the ball. Even though the wood has changed shape and therefore physical properties, the chemical nature of the wood has not been altered. The bat and the original piece of wood are still the same chemical substance

Looking at the above scripture in Ecclesiastes, we can see that the almighty God has set things in place thus physical changes will always occur in the human race. For us it means that there is a time to be born and a time to die. When we are born we go through what we call the human cycle: from birth, toddler, infant, adolescent, to adulthood and death. It is important for us to remember that anything that has got a beginning has got an end. In other words, once you have been born, it is a sign that one day you will die and leave this earth. Now the question you should ask yourself is where will you spend eternity?

One can only know and understand these respective times, if one properly 'walks after the spirit'. In Romans 8:1, 'This can be done only by the believer exhibiting faith in Christ as the source, and the cross as the means, and maintaining his faith in that capacity'. This means that the Holy Spirit works entirely within the framework of the finished work of Christ. He demands of us, which is precious little to demand, that our faith ever be in that finished work. That being done, the spirit of God will work in our lives, leading and guiding us. Check John 16:13-15, Romans 8:2, 11. KJV

> ***★ 'When we least expect it, life sets us a challenge to test our courage and willingness to change; at such a moment, there is no point in pretending that nothing has happened or in saying that we are not yet ready. The challenge will not wait. Life does not look back. A week is more than enough time for us to decide whether or not to accept our destiny.'***
>
> ***– Paulo Coelho, The Devil and Miss Prym***
>
> ★★★★★★★★

Dealing with the issue of physical change, the question we ask ourselves again is how do we handle it? The earlier ages of one's life look perfect but, as you age, changes begin to occur. You start seeing wrinkles both on your face and body, grey hair and not being able to do what you used to do or eat what you used to eat. I know most people, especially women, do not want to see that at all to the extent of some having plastic surgery to delay the signs of ageing. But the fact of the matter is that nature cannot be cheated. It will one day show up. However, not all people react in this way because some do not mind what happens to their physical body, in other words they are proud of the changes because it shows how long they have been in existence. For these people, it is fantastic to be able to advise the younger generation by turning 'the hearts of the fathers to the children and the hearts of the children to the fathers' (Malachi 4:5, 6. KJV).

Economical Change

An economic downturn or change suggests the economy is entering into recession. A recession is a period of negative economic growth with falling output and rising unemployment. The official definition of a recession is negative economic growth for two consecutive quarters. The definition of an economic downturn is less strict. For example, many felt we were in an economic downturn even with positive growth. This was because the growth rate was slowing down, house prices were falling and people could see the economic cycle shifting from a boom period and towards bust.

Let us now look to the main features of an economic downturn:

- Negative or very low economic growth
- Rising unemployment
- Falling asset prices - shares and house prices
- Low confidence and falling investment

- Rising spare capacity
- Increasing government borrowing

We may experience the changes in an economic downturn but we must also remember that we came to this world with nothing and we will take nothing away says the Holy Bible. The question however remains: does God promise us financial prosperity? This question has been and always will be. Finding an answer to such a question requires that one should explore the original intent of God concerning blessing His children with financial wealth. Having known the original intent, the next is the purpose of it.

It is true that in the Hebrew scriptures, we often find God's blessing associated with material prosperity. For example, Deuteronomy 8:18, which is my favourite scripture, says 'You must remember the Lord your God, because He gives you the power to get wealth'. The power to get wealth that the author of Hebrew is trying to explain is the enabling force and blessing behind what brings wealth. This assured the Israelites that if they were obedient to God, He would make them a prosperous nation. This obedience applied to all God's children including this generation and to you, who are reading this book.

It is stated in the book of Malachi 3:10, 'Bring ye all tithes and offering into my house, that they might be meat in my house and test me that I would not open the window of heaven and pour you out a blessing that you will not have enough room to store. And I would rebuke the devourer for your sake'. Giving tithe and offering to God will not automatically result in getting a corresponding financial wealth, rather, the blessing will open up heaven to pour down 'dews of heaven' which is a conducive environment that makes all things grow and prosper. If your business is growing, with God's protection, without any losses or bad financial decisions, financial wealth and prosperity are guaranteed.

The Kingdom of God operates on principles and is not a respecter of persons or religion. Anyone that starts obeying these principles will automatically enjoy the financial prosperity that God promises. True financial prosperity is experienced when the purpose of it is for Kingdom expansion. This is true of individuals in the bible. The faithful man Job was enormously wealthy, and after Satan brought him to abject poverty, God in His manifold wisdom, after Job had prayed for his friends, gave and restored to him twice as much as he had before. (Job 1:3, 42:10). Abraham too was wealthy, stocked with herds, silver, gold and slaves. There are men and women of God that did experience great wealth namely but few Abraham, Jacob, Isaac, Solomon, David other unnamed individuals such as Joseph of Arimathea who later requested the body of Jesus to be buried in his tomb.

Being in a position of great wealth is enormously beneficial but what about a sudden change in your economic circumstances? How do you deal with that? As stated previously, change is inevitable and there are so many changes we humans go through: marital, psychological, emotional, political, social cultural, and relationships to mention a few. How do you deal with such changes? This is what this book is about i.e. to give you insight to some of these changes and to acquaint you with Bible strategies that will help you manage the changes.

Above all, have faith in God who is able to keep your soul from destruction and who can restore every lost thing in your life. As you read this book and follow some of the Bible guidelines you will see the God of Breakthrough working in your life today.

Managing Change

Change management is a systematic approach to dealing with change, both from the perspective of an organisation and on the individual level. A somewhat ambiguous term, change management has at least three different aspects, including: adapting to change, controlling change, and effecting change. A proactive approach to dealing with change is at the core of all three aspects. For an organisation, change management means defining and implementing procedures and/or technologies to deal with changes in the business environment and to profit from changing opportunities.

Successful adaptation to change is as crucial within an organisation as it is in the natural world. Just like plants and animals, organisations and the individuals in them inevitably encounter changing conditions that they are powerless to control. The more effectively you deal with change, the more likely you are to thrive. Adaptation might involve establishing a structured methodology for responding to changes in the business environment (such as a fluctuation in the economy, or a threat from a competitor) or establishing coping mechanisms for responding to changes in the workplace (such as new policies, or technologies).

Terry Paulson, the author of *Paulson on Change*, quotes an uncle's advice: 'It's easiest to ride a horse in the direction it is going.' In other words, don't struggle against change; learn to use it to your advantage.[1]

It becomes easy and possible when you allow yourself to change in the direction of change and whilst going through change, lessons must be learnt to use it in the next level of life. Effectively managing change can result in growth of any form. However, questions must be asked as to what kind of change one expects. What are the benefits that would be derived from the change? Who is going to be affected by the change and, should something go wrong, how are you going to resolve and rectify it quickly?

Change should not be forced on people and must be **SMART.**

S – Simple
M – Measurable
A – Achievable
R – Realistic
T – Time bound.

It also means that, for effective change to take place, it has to be in line with the vision of the company or the individual for an achievable goal. Also, change process must be well communicated to avoid confusion

---

[1] http://searchcio.techtarget.com/definition/change-management

and ambiguity at all levels. In other words, it must be clear from the onset what it's all about.

Summary

Rightly said above, change is inevitable and no one can resist change. Any attempt to resist change can result in fatality of one's own progress and advancement in life. Whatever change that may occur in one's life definitely will not be permanent. Understanding this paradoxical revelation will transform your life. Change from all perspective is natural to existence and common to everyone. It also reveals the fact that man is finite and everything created has its own seasons and times and nothing on earth will be forever. Anything that has got a beginning has an end.

Many people without this understanding about change worry a lot. However, if we could accept the fact that nothing in life is going to be permanent, life will bring such an awesome peace to mankind. If this happens, then we will not be surprised when something in our life changes, be they physical changes, spiritual changes, economical changes and so on and so forth.

CHAPTER 2
Elijah's Survival Strategies - 1Kings 17:1-16

Let us take a quick look at Elijah's life for it would be inappropriate to write about his strategies without introducing this great man of God, whose legacy is alive today and still being studied.

> ***★ 'Stepping onto a brand-new path is difficult, but not more difficult than remaining in a situation, which is not nurturing to the whole woman.'***
>
> ***– Maya Angelou***
>
> 

In 1Kings 17:1 'And Elijah the Tishbite, who was of the inhabitants of Gilead, said unto Ahab, As the Lord God of Israel liveth, before whom I stand, there shall not be dew nor rain these years, but according to my word'. What a profound declaration from this great man of God! He was so sure about his calling and ministry and, more so, his divine identity and the authority that he carried on Planet Earth.

Elijah knew what I call the rules of engagement and he was really effecting Genesis 1:28 'and let them have dominion...'. He knew that nothing happens on this earth until man who has been placed here legally speaks out. This was the original plan or intent of our Heavenly Father. Matthew 18:18 'Very very I say unto you (Man, Elijah, You that you are reading this book), whatsoever ye shall bind on earth shall be bound in heaven: and whatsoever things ye shall loose shall be loosed in heaven'.

As humans we are placed here on earth to rule and have dominion over the earth, not another fellow human being. That was the instruction God gave to Adam in the Garden of Eden. If today's believers are able to identify their divine mandate and exercise it, no demon powers will be able to stand against it. Hallelujah to the King of Kings. Shout amen to that.

There were a lot of miracles that God wrought with the hands of Elijah and we will look at some of them later on. Elijah's commitment to God was phenomenal and challenges us today. He was sent to confront and speak out as he hears it from God to a King who always rejects His instruction. This great man of God took a decision to carry his ministry or life assignment alone and, by so doing, experienced isolation from others but he remained faithful to God. He went through changes and situations that we are going through today. Elijah trusted God fully. He who called him (Elijah) into the ministry is faithful to accomplish His plans.

Elijah took his time to know God and His ways and observed them accordingly and made his way prosperous. For example, after God worked an overwhelming miracle through him in defeating the Baal prophets, Queen Jezebel retaliated by threatening Elijah's life. Elijah ran for his life although he was a man of God. He felt fearful, depressed and rejected. In spite of God's provision for him he still wanted to die.

This is exactly the type of change we might have experienced. What we need to remember is that all we need is provided by God. More often than not change brings confusion that sometimes we want to throw in the towel and say enough is enough. In as much as Elijah wanted to die, God showed him many things to prove He is in control but never spoke it loudly; rather He chose to speak in a still, small voice. In our world today, we seem to struggle to hear the voice of God due to too much noise around us.

Elijah struggled with his feelings even after his comforting message from God. So God confronted Elijah's emotions and demanded action from him. He told Elijah that the changes he was going through and his loneliness was due to his ignorance as 7,000 others in Israel were still faithful to God. Oh! How often we lose focus on what God is doing and the fact that He is still faithful today. Hosea 4:6 'Lack of knowledge my people perish'.

Even today, God still speaks through the quiet and obvious rather than the spectacular and unusual. God has work for us to do even when we feel fear and failure. God always has more resources and people than we know; although we might wish to do amazing miracles for God, we should instead focus on developing a personal relationship with Him. The real miracles Elijah and others experience in the Bible are due to their personal relationship with God. If we can develop a good and personal relationship with God the Father, Son and Holy Spirit we shall experience greater miracles than Elijah and the rest experienced.

Read John 14:12 'Very truly I say to you, he that believes in me (Jesus) the works I do shall he (You) also do, even GREATER WORKS shall he do; because I go to my father'.

In Act 10:38 'How God anointed Jesus Christ of Nazareth with the Holy Spirit and power and how He went about doing good healing the sick because God was with Him'.

You see, all the above happened due to their personal relationship with God. Do you have a personal relationship with God? If you do, at what level?

Let us look as some of the accomplishments or the miracles God used Elijah to achieve.

1. He predicted drought (1 Kings 17: 1)
2. He restored a boy to life (1 King 17:17 – 24)
3. He rebuked King Ahab (1 King 18:1-15)
4. He represented God in a showdown with priests of Baal and Asherah (1Kings 18:16 – 40)
5. Appeared with Moses and Jesus in the New Testament transfiguration scene

In the account of this great man of God, we realise that he was chosen to do God's work alone which resulted in isolation, loneliness and fear from Jezebel when she threatened his life. We are to learn from this experience that it is not good to be alone or work alone. A network of people is really healthy and we must encourage it. We are never closer to defeat than at our moment of greatest victory. We must also understand and be alert to the fact that God speaks more frequently in persistent whispers than in shouts.

Although, we are not told who his parents were, Elijah's story is throughout the Bible. Let us takes a brief moment to study a few.

2Chronicles 21:12 – 15;

'And there came a writing to him from Elijah the prophet, saying, Thus saith the LORD God of David thy father, Because thou hast not walked in the ways of Jehoshaphat thy father, nor in the ways of Asa king of Judah', 2Ki 2:1

13 'But hast walked in the way of the kings of Israel, and hast made Judah and the inhabitants of Jerusalem to go a whoring, like to the whoredoms of the house of Ahab, and also hast slain thy brethren of thy father's house, which were better than thyself':

Ex 34:15; De 31:16; 1Ki 16:31-33; 2Ki 9:22; 2Ch 21:4,11

14 'Behold, with a great plague will the LORD smite thy people, and thy children, and thy wives, and all thy goods.

15 'And thou shalt have great sickness by disease of thy bowels, until thy bowels fall out by reason of the sickness day by day'.

Malachi 4:5-6;

5 'Behold, I will send you Elijah the prophet before the coming of the great and dreadful day of the LORD:

Joel 2:31; Matthew 11:14; 17:11; Mark 9:11; Luke 1:17

6 'And he shall turn the heart of the fathers to the children, and the heart of the children to their fathers, lest I come and smite the earth with a curse'.

Zec 5:3; 14:12

Luke 1:17

17 'And he shall go before him in the spirit and power of Elias, to turn the hearts of the fathers to the children, and the disobedient to the wisdom of the just; to make ready a people prepared for the Lord'.

Malachi 4:5; Matthew 11:14; Mark 9:12

Romans 11:2-4

2 'God hath not cast away his people which he foreknew. Do ye not what the scripture saith of Elias? How he maketh intercession to God against Israel.

Romans 8:29

3 'Lord, they have killed thy prophets, and digged down thine altars; and I am left alone, and they seek my life'.

1Kings 19:10,14

4 'But what saith the answer of God unto him? I have reserved to myself seven thousand men, who have not bowed the knee to the image of Baal'.

James 5:17

17 'Elias was a man subject to like passions as we are, and he prayed earnestly that it might not rain: and it rained not on the earth by the space of three years and six months.

1King 17:1; Luke 4:25; Acts 14:15

18 'And he prayed again, and the heaven gave rain, and the earth brought forth her fruit'.

1Kings 18:42,45

Season of Change has Begun

Elijah was one of the first in a long line of important prophets God sent to Israel and Judah. Israel, the Northern Kingdom, had no faithful kings throughout its history. Each king was wicked and disobedient to God. God chose Elijah to become a prophet to speak to the nation Israel and Judah in the absence of a faithful king to lead the people in worshipping God. Few priests were left from the tribe of Levi and the priests appointed by Israel's kings were corrupt and ineffective. The reason why God chose prophets or would choose a prophet in the absence of a king was to bring them from their moral and spiritual decline. These men and women play a vital role in the history of God's people by encouraging the people, directing them and leading them back to God.

Test of Elijah's Ministry Authority

Every called leader of God would go through a moment of test or trial of leadership and authority to prove and to establish the authentic calling. An ability to survive the test and trial would give the so-called leader a lid or an edge over the followers. As a leader or man of God, know this for certain: depending upon the level of your spiritual maturity, level of anointing and the purpose and destination of your calling, would determine the type of attack or demon that Satan would release. Remember in the case of Adam and Eve and also Jesus, Satan came himself.

In the case of the Prophet Elijah, many are the tests he went through to establish the prophetic calling of God upon his life. But for the sake of this book, we shall look into basically one of the major tests. Not only did he survive it but rather proved to King Ahab and his evil wife Jezebel that there is still a God in Israel. Let us read it for ourselves.

1 Kings 16:29 – 34.

Ahab Becomes King of Israel

29 'In the thirty-eighth year of Asa king of Judah, Ahab son of Omri became king of Israel, and he reigned in Samaria over Israel twenty-two years. **30**
Ahab son of Omri did more evil in the eyes of the LORD than any of those before him. **31** He not only
considered it trivial to commit the sins of Jeroboam son of Nebat, but he also married Jezebel, daughter of Ethbaal king of the Sidonians, and began to serve Baal and worship him. **32** He set up an altar for Baal in the
temple of Baal that he built in Samaria. **33** Ahab also
made an Asherah pole and did more to provoke the LORD, the God of Israel, to anger than did all the kings of Israel before him. **34** In Ahab's time, Hiel of
Bethel rebuilt Jericho. He laid its foundations at the cost of his firstborn son Abiram, and he set up its gates at the cost of his youngest son Segub, in accordance with the word of the LORD spoken by Joshua son of Nun'.

We can see in the above scriptures, Elijah the prophet ministry sprang directly under a king called Ahab who married an evil wife, Jezebel, who gradually led the King and the entire nation to worship idols. Jezebel came from the Phoenician city of Tyre where her father had been a high priest and eventually king; Jezebel worshipped the god Baal. In order to please her, King Ahab built a temple and an altar for Baal, thus promoting idolatry and leading the entire nation into sin. This later provoked God. He said in His word, 'I am the God of jealousy I do not share my glory with anyone' and in the ten commandments He said, 'Do not worship any other God except the maker of heaven and earth'. What King Ahab did greatly annoyed God and He decided not to take it any longer by calling His servant Elijah to speak the truth. He could not do this except by letting the man of God prophesy which will later prove that there is a God in Israel and also established Elijah's calling and ministry.

1 Kings 17:1-16

Elijah's Prophecy and Strategies Adopted

1 'Now Elijah the Tishbite, from Tishbe in Gilead, said to Ahab, 'As the LORD, the God of Israel, lives, whom I serve, there will be neither dew nor rain in the next few years except at my word.'

The man of God Elijah opened his mouth and declared and decreed to King Ahab, his wife and entire nation 'there shall be no rain except by my word'. God honours His faithful servants' words. He used the same principles and strategies in creating the world. Words are very powerful and we are to be mindful of how we use them. Elijah's own words drove him into the wilderness and it took God's grace to save him. Many a time you hear young men and women calling on God to anoint and use them and some of this anointing can take you to your personal wilderness. The Bible says after John the Baptist baptised Jesus in the River Jordan, the spirit (Anointing) came upon Jesus like a dove and straight away from there He (Jesus) went into the wilderness for forty days and forty nights where he fasted and prayed.

Proverbs 13:2, 'From the fruit of his lips a man enjoys good things, but the unfaithful have a craving for violence.

Proverbs 12:14, 'From the fruit of his lips a man is filled with good things as surely as the work of his hands rewards him'.

You have within you the power to make your life what you desire it to be. Your spoken word is not only powerful to make changes in your life; it is the power through which definite changes come about. Regardless of outside influences, you shape your life through your thoughts and words. You do this whether or not you are aware of it.

When you know the power of words, especially your spoken words, you will put a guard at your lips and be very wise in what words pass through. You will do the same with your ears in that you will allow only that which is uplifting, positive and life-enriching to enter and find lodging in your thought process.

Words Mould and Shape Your Life

Words can make your life miserable or marvellous, it is up to you. Just as what you think makes you what you are, words mould and shape your life because words are the expressions of thought, ideas held in mind. Negative words result in negative, unhappy experiences. Positive words result in positive, happy and prosperous experiences. Therefore, watch what comes out of your mouth. God actually created the universe by the words of His mouth. The scripture says, the abundance of the heart the mouth speaks. What has your heart been conceiving? Before you speak, think about what you are going to say. If it's edifying go ahead and if not do not do it as you will be reaping exactly what comes out of your mouth. More so, watch your thought pattern. Some thoughts come in mind uninvited and they are the ones if not checked or put under control can jeopardise our destiny. Jesus was walking with His disciples, feeling hungry, when he saw a fig tree with its leaves looking green and thought He might get fruits to eat. Surprisingly, it wasn't time for the fig tree to bear fruit and Jesus opened His mouth, spoke to the fig for not bearing fruit anymore and they moved on. Amazingly, the day after, coming along the same road the disciples saw the fig tree Jesus spoke against the previous day had withered. They drew His attention to it and He opened His mouth and said, have faith in God for whatever you say with your

'Those who cannot change their minds cannot change anything.'

– George Bernard Shaw

mouth will come to pass. Honestly speaking, if words are powerful in altering our lives, then we have to say the things we only want to see happening in our lives. Declaring and decreeing must be the order of the day for believers and anyone who want to see positive change in his or her life must begin to speak and confess the positive things he or she want to see.

What You Declare Makes a Difference

In speaking words, you are literally moving substance, making a definite difference somewhere in some way. Most of all, you are making a definite, although seemingly imperceptible, difference within yourself and upon the conditions of your life. That is why there is specific benefit to you when you consciously and deliberately make prospering declarations by using the affirmations from God's word. Your mountains have got ears and they only know your voice. By speaking to those mountains they are automatically removed out of your life. Jesus said, 'You will emphasise what you will say to this mountain: 'Be thou removed and go yonder and it will obey you'.

Divine Strategies

2 Then the word of the LORD came to Elijah:

In verses 2 you see God speaking to Elijah by giving him the strategies or specific instructions for what he should be doing; in other words, to go through the changes that are occurring. This is where most believers struggle. When we are going through changes in our life in any form whether created by our own words or created by somebody else, the most important thing is the ability to hear from God. The art of hearing God's voice in our noisy society is a must for us to develop if we are willing to live as redeemed Christians of our God. Having said that, the Christian faith is a journey or a race set before us. (Hebrews 12:1), 'Therefore, we are to run with all diligence and not be weary. In running, we sometimes feel tired, weak, dry and lonely and some people give up entirely to pursue the pleasures of this life which last but for a moment, and sorrow follows.'

We deal with the challenges or changes of this life differently when someone is with us than we do if we are alone. All of us sometime need companionship. Sometimes we desire to see a miracle or some other sign from God to confirm He is with us and willing to direct us. Hearing from God requires a diligent search and act of faith through personal spiritual attentiveness and personal quiet time. Do not also lose the fact that if we ask Him to help us hear Him speak to us He will. Amen.

The Place Called 'There'

One cannot and must not be at all places to receive divine visitation but rather be at the right place at the right time to meet the right people. Throughout scripture, there is always a place called 'THERE' that God has always prepared for His children who obey His voice and have chosen to follow His will for their lives.

'There' the Lord has commanded His blessing. Read Psalm 133. There I have commanded the ravens; There I have commanded the widow to feed you.

Never rush to place or even join a Church because you see people are being blessed there or receiving something. Make sure God is leading you to the place. If that is where God has prepared for you, 'There' will be provision. Lack is a sign of being at the wrong place at the right time. There are many people the Lord asked them to leave a particular place to go to another place for His direction and provision. Examples are Abraham, Isaac, Jacob, Paul, the apostles and our Lord Jesus. You can also see that our Lord could not do well in certain places. Don't walk in wrong counsel. Do not follow blindly. We have only one life and do not experiment in the wilderness of nowhere. It's too costly.

Everyone has been designed for a specific environment in which to function. Once you are out of your environment you struggle to function. Fishes are for water. Birds are for the air. The sun does not struggle to shine because built in it lies the ability to shine in its domain. What environment has been designed for you? Are you in the right kind of business or trade? Are you studying the right course? Do not take up a job because of the size of the salary but choose a course or a job based on your calling or destiny.

Start looking for the place called 'THERE' for your life, family, ministry and business. Can it be that your marriage, family, business etc is struggling due to the fact that you are at the wrong place? Well, I cannot answer for you but rather seek the one who created you.

Ironically, many folks are in wrong courses, careers, jobs, business, marriages and even churches and all that they do is complain about not being happy due to someone or something trivial. Let me emphasise here by saying if there is anything you are unhappy about, it can be a clue you have been wired or designed to solve it which can a clue to your calling but be sure of it before embarking on any journey in correcting it. Complaining too much will not solve any problem. Just get up and get yourself in your environment.

Summary

As a man of God, Elijah looked up and watched ravens feed him from the skies and drank from the Brook Cherith. Although Jewish traditions considered them to be unclean birds, Elijah did not care who brought the meat.

He also saw people die of hunger, but what could he do? He, himself, did not know that his own prophecy could even drive him into the wilderness. How amazing and surprising to find oneself in a place of little help or no help at all. We are encouraged throughout scripture; we should always look up to heaven for supplies.

God is able to turn our predicament into testimonies for His glory. We can argue that God fed Elijah which is very true according to the passage. But one will realise, it was not only the supply from heaven but being at the right place at the right time for divine provision. Elijah never followed his desires or will but actually waited patiently for God's direction of where the next food would come from. The Will of God will not take you to a place where His grace will not keep you. Provision can be a sign that you are at the right place.

CHAPTER 3
Strategies

Survival has always been man's strategy to existence. To live fulfilling and productive lives, we should discover how to manage changes that occur to us. Secondly, how to come out very strong after the change that occurred and benefit from it. Bearing this in mind, lead us to study some of the strategies Elijah adopted during his time not only to survive but triumph. We cannot do this without actually looking into the word strategy, what it means and how to apply it during periods of change.

The word *strategy* derives from the Greek word *strategos* which translates to the art of the general. This is often confused with tactics, from the Greek *taktike*. *Taktike* translates as organising an army. In modern usage, strategy and tactics might refer not only to warfare but to a variety of business practices. Essentially, strategy is the thinking aspect of planning a change, organising something or planning a war. Strategy lays out the goals that need to be accomplished and the ideas for achieving those goals. Strategy can be complex, multi-layered plans for accomplishing objectives and may give consideration to tactics.Tactics are the meat and bread of the strategy. They are the 'doing' aspect that follows the planning. Tactics refer specifically to action. In the strategy phase of a plan, the thinkers decide how to achieve their goals; in other words, they think about how people will act. They decide on what tactics will be employed to fulfil the strategy.

Strategy 1: Hide Yourself

3. 'Leave here, turn eastward and hide in the Kerith Ravine, east of the Jordan. 4 You will drink from the brook, and I have ordered the ravens to feed you there'.

Anytime there is a change in our situation or circumstance such as those experienced by the man of God, Elijah, we often look for an exit plan or strategy. Remember that the best strategist is God who is able to make all grace abound. In the case of Elijah, although he caused the problem to prove the existence of God, God supported his actions and provided a strategy for him to survive the change that had occurred by his own very words.

Ladies and gentlemen, notice here the change that occurred was not caused by Satan and his numerous demons who are useless and powerless in all sense. This change and trouble was caused by Elijah and God. Many times when believers are going through a little bit of change or challenges, we start blaming the devil or a family relative for our calamities. There are times when God will bring a sudden change into your life, not to destroy you but give you a promotion out of it. Remember, God will not tempt you to commit sin but He will trial you especially when you have been sitting in your comfort zone for a long time.

He said in Haggai 2:6-9, This is what the LORD Almighty says: 'In a little while I will once more shake the heavens and the earth, the sea and the dry land. **7** I will shake all nations, and the desired of all nations will come, and I will fill this house with glory,' says the LORD Almighty. **8** 'The silver is mine and the gold is mine,' declares the LORD Almighty. **9** 'The glory of this present house will be greater than the glory of the former house,' says the LORD Almighty. 'And in this place I will grant peace,' declares the LORD Almighty.' This is true, He does this to bring glory to His name and His house. Amen

Whenever you are going through any kind of change in your life the first questions you need to ask are who is behind this change and what caused it? You do this by praying, reading the scriptures and being still to hear His still small voice. Do not get me wrong if I say be very careful with the so-called End time prophet who only prophecy for their stomach and create a whole lot of confusion among family members and relatives. Doesn't make sense, please explain. On the other hand, there are genuine prophets God is using to give direction in life. Only use this at the last resort.

In the case of Elijah, the change was caused by His own spoken words. God honours you when the situation becomes unbearable. This was also the case for Elijah who sought God's direction and counsel. God not only gave Elijah strategies to survive the change but also used it as an opportunity to bless a widow who is later mentioned by Jesus in the gospel of Luke.

The first strategic plan God gave to Elijah is, **leave (Movement)** and **hide (minimise)** yourself in a place I have chosen for you. I will deal with the leave (movement) later but now let us focus on the hiding. Let us apply this to economic change; one must not continue spending money that you don't have. Instead it is better to cut down on expenditure and try as much as possible to spend within your means. In other words, minimise everything to a level you can handle.

Practical Advice

1. Start planning ahead

With talk of an economic recession or downturn looming, we should not wait and then decide what to do. Begin planning now for the possibility of things getting worse. A period of economic decline or indeed any kind of decline or slowdown is very real. In other words, we may experience this type of change as a form of suffering. So I say, forget about what people are saying or what the news is telling you and begin to look at things from your own perspective or from God's perspective.

If you feel you're doing all right financially, then plan ahead for the possibility that things may take a turn for the worse. If you're already suffering financially then start thinking about how to handle it if it lasts longer or gets worse.

2. You're not alone

A change in circumstances such as financial change affects many people! So take some comfort in knowing you are, by far, not alone. The reason I mention this is to help ease your level of stress. If you're suffering financially, others are too!

But to survive, you cannot brood over it and let it take over your life. Why not? Because that will make you even more depressed and do more harm than good. So just look at it from the perspective that others are in the same position and sometimes worse off than you. Yet, life goes on.

The economy goes through ups and down, so we all in our lifetime experience this kind of change.

3. Know your income and expenses

> ***'To win one hundred victories in one hundred battles is not the acme of skill. To subdue the enemy without fighting is the acme of skill'***
>
> ***– Sun Tzu, The Art of War***
>
> ★★★★★★★

There are many of us who know how much we're bringing home in pay and other sources of income. But many people don't realise how much they're spending. Of course we know the major expenses such as rent or mortgage, utilities, car and student loans. But the 'little ones', the smaller amounts of money spent can often really eat up your savings and take-home pay!

So step 1, make an accurate list of what you take in (income); exactly what you spend it on (expenses); track all your expenses, not just the 'biggies'.

This means including things like coffee, pastries, partying, movies and rentals, gas, etc. As I said before, these are the ones that really add-up and eat into your savings. Most people are shocked at how much they're really spending when they see this list.

4. Debt is the enemy

Debt is money that you owe, meaning bills. Now there are 'good bills' and 'bad bills'. The good ones are those that are necessities i.e. rent and utilities because in order to live, you have no choice but to spend money on these.

But where we get ourselves into trouble is with the bad ones. These are the luxuries and frills: why spend on a 52-inch plasma television when a 20-inch flat or round screen (regular television) will do; the same applies to spending £1000 on a computer when one bought for £200 will do the job.

Credit card debt is the true evil that gets most of us into major league trouble! We tend to look at this as 'free money'. However, it's not our money; it belongs to the credit card company. Avoiding this fact will make us overspend and live way beyond our means.

So, control your credit card debt to the hilt. If the credit card company wants to raise your limit, don't go out and spend it. Just because you have a £6000 limit doesn't mean you have to spend it. Only use it when absolutely necessary!

5. Debit cards

As opposed to credit cards, debit cards work a bit differently. The major difference is that they aren't loans like credit cards! When you use a debit card, money is taken out directly from your bank account. So if you don't have it in your account, it's unavailable. This gives people a huge dose of reality and helps control spending. Why? Put simply, you won't spend it if you don't have it. If you do use it then you can easily see your balance dropping.

With credit cards, you don't have to worry about money being taken out of your bank account immediately. Nor do you have to pay the full amount when the bill comes. You can pay the minimum - a measly £20-30 for example. And that's how you get yourself into financial trouble. Because you look at it this way!

And of course, credit card companies will raise your limit even if you have lousy credit, which encourages people to overspend. After all, you only have to pay the minimum and credit card companies know that this can drag on for 100 years, if you let it. Think of the outrageous interest rates! So you're like gold to them. Don't fall for it and cater to them!

Furthermore, if you have a debit card with the Visa or Mastercard logo, then it can work just like a credit card in the sense that stores can swipe them as they would a credit card. In addition, you can withdraw money from ATM machines without the cash advance fees associated with credit cards. Many banks don't charge ATM fees if you use your debit card at their branches. This helps save you even more money!

6. Pay down debt

Let's say you have £15,000 in credit card debt and pay £30 a month towards it. If you increase your payment, even a little bit, you'll save lots of money in the end! And that's because the interest you're accruing is being reduced.

You see, it's not the £15,000 that's the trouble. It's the never-ending interest being added to it that really gets most people. Even with a low interest rate, you're still accruing it and paying it every single time you send in a partial payment. So increasing your payment amounts by a little or a lot more will cut your interest and get your debt paid off much sooner!

This same principle applies to all forms of debt: car loans, student loans, personal loans, etc.

With debit cards, you don't have to worry about this because no interest is accruing! When you use the card, the full amount is immediately deducted. So if you spend £100, then £100 is taken out.

7. Eat in and cook at home

You'd be surprised at how much you can save by eating in! It's far less expensive to buy food at the store and cook it at home than to eat out. Now by buying food, I don't mean a ready-made meal that you reheating at home. I mean buying ingredients such as meat, fish and vegetables that you'll cook to make soups and pasta dishes. If you buy the things you really like in bulk, that will save you even more money. For example, at my local supermarket, I can get four packs of six pasta noodles for just £5.99. With each pasta noodle being a meal, it means I could cook 24 meals for under £6! So you'll save a good deal of money by eating more at home and it's less costly than going to McDonalds, Burger King, or other restaurants (fast-food and non fast-food)!

Now I'm not saying you should eat in all the time, unless you want to. Just by swapping one home-cooked meal for a non-home-cooked one will save you money. You can do the same at work. Instead of eating out every day, take in your food once in a while or every day.

8. Reduce drinks

Instead of buying sodas or juices, try drinking tap water or fill a bottle with water from a drinking fountain at work. As I mentioned in step 7, you can do this once in a while or every time. Either way, you'll save money by drinking water instead of having to spend on soda or juice.

As an alternative, if you want more flavour, drink tea or coffee. With coffee, you get lots of drinks out of one container. With tea, you can get more than one cup of tea out of one teabag. Some people manage to get up to four cups of tea from a single bag!

If you really want to drink a coffee from places such as Starbucks where the drinks are quite expensive, try to reduce the size of your drink. If you normally drink a large coffee, try a small one. This is especially helpful for those of you who like Starbucks and other coffee houses. Other things you can try are: reducing the number of shots of coffee in a drink; swapping an expensive drink such as triple grande mocha for a cheaper one such as a latte; passing on a syrup flavouring that adds to the cost of your drink. One last alternative is to pass on buying a drink from time to time. In other words, if you're getting something every day, don't do it one day.So you can see that there are many ways to cut down the amount you spend on drinks and every little bit you save helps you ride out the economic hard times! Remember, it's the little bits you save here and there that really add up to lots!Folk, I believe I have done a little bit of justice on coping with financial change. There is other practical advice available from experts on any form of change one is going through but I have realised the most challenging one is our economic stability. Anytime Satan wants to attack a believer, his first strategy is to attack his or her finances and all other vices will follow. It is my prayer that the God who supplies our needs according to His riches in glory by Christ Jesus will breakthrough on all fronts and bring you financial deliverance. Amen.

Strategy 2: Mental Shift

'5 So he did what the LORD had told him. He went to the Kerith Ravine, east of the Jordan, and stayed there. 6 The ravens brought him bread and meat in the morning

and bread and meat in the evening, and he drank from the brook'.

The next strategic plan God gave to Elijah was to go through what I call mental shift or adjustment. Ravens were seen to be unclean birds and despite the fact that ravens love meat, God still used them in feeding and keeping His servant alive. Beloved, when the season changes, one needs to go through some kind of mental shift or adjustment to survive the change. In the case of Elijah, he could have said ravens were unclean birds so he would not have eaten the food they brought for him. However, he said to himself, 'The season has changed and there is no way can obtain food so whether ravens or whoever brings the food, I will eat it'. What this teaches us is that there are things you would not eat but when the season changes, we must go through a mental shift because the alternative is starvation and death. There are people you do not associate with but when the season changes, you go through a mental shift and start associating to survive the change. The word of God says, 'The wealth of the wicked will be laid down for the Just'. You see, God can use unbelievers to supply your needs in order for you to survive a seasonal change in your life. Therefore, do not resist the move of God and do not criticise when God is at work. On the other hand one needs to be careful not to become involved in the activities of sinners.

> ***'We do not place especial value on the possession of a virtue until we notice its total absence in our opponent.'***
>
> ***– Friedrich Nietzsche***
>
> 

Practical Advice

Jesus in His last speech gave us all what we call 'The Great Commission'. Jesus said, 'Go ye to all the nations, preaching and teaching the good news, baptising them in the name of the Father, the Son and the Holy Spirit'. Amen. As a missionary or an ambassador of Christ, you might have travelled to a place where most of the people are unbelievers, for example, an employer may be an atheist but you know that the only way to survive economically is to take the job. If you do not go through a mental shift and take up a job offer from that unbeliever you might not be able to survive.

Strategy 3: Movements

7 'Some time later the brook dried up because there had been no rain in the land. 8 Then the word of the LORD came to him: 9 'Go at once to Zarephath of Sidon and stay there. I have commanded a widow in that place to supply you with food.'

Our God is not a static God but rather a dynamic God. In His third strategic plan for Elijah, He caused Elijah to move from one place to other. Where He directs there will always be provision. May I announce to you, dear friend, if you are in a place where provision is short it might be that God is directing you to a new place of provision and you need to urgently get on your knees to seek for His next place. In the following verses I want to introduce to you how God instructed Elijah to move from one place to another in other to survive the change.

- 1 Kings 17:2-3 = **2** then the word of the LORD came to Elijah: **3 'Leave here**, turn eastward and hide in the Kerith Ravine, east of the Jordan.'
- 1 Kings 17:8 = **8** Then the word of the LORD came to him: **9 'Go at once to Zarephath** in the region of Sidon and stay there. I have directed a widow there to supply you with food.'

From the above scriptures you will find out that when Elijah prophesied, he thought he would still be enjoying supplies from heaven. Little did he know that his own prophesy would drive him into the wilderness. At times many Christians pray for or begin to say or prophesy in their prayers and when their prayers drive them into the desert of their lives they begin to question the integrity of God's word. Maybe you are reading this book of prophecy right now and your life looks like you are in the wilderness of your life. Check some prayers you have prayed before and ask God to give you an exit strategy.

Elijah was living in his comfort zone when he prophesied. God asked him to move from Gilead and turn to eastward to the brook Cherith, east of Jordan. The brook dried again and God showed up and asked him to move to Zarephath in the region of Sidon and stay there. In all these places because God directed Elijah to go there, He always made provision for his survival.

Practical Advice

1. In an economic down time, if a business wants to survive and bounce back strongly, it should be

looking into moving its offices abroad or outsource some of its businesses in order to get cash flowing. Some firms think of merging two positions.

2. On the other hand, a small or medium sized company might be struggling to compete with the bigger companies in town for the market share. If the small to medium sized company would move to a suburb and reduce its operating and fixed costs, the chances of getting its market share, facing little or no competition at all, would be a great deal.

3. If a small Church or minister is struggling with all this bigger Churches and well-known TV evangelists and losing all his souls to them, that Church or minister should be thinking of moving to a small village nearby for survival. In such a place, people might not have the opportunity to see all the well-known TV evangelists and the only person they might see is you.

4. A young man or woman at the age of marriage might be struggling to find a life partner in the city or abroad. If you obey the voice of God and move to the village or hinterland you might be regarded as the next beauty queen/king in town and you would marry the best man or woman there.

5. A young graduate might be earning more money but his/her skills and ability are underutilised at work. It would be a very good idea to move to a new firm which might pay you less but would make very good use of your skills and ability.

6. A graduate with a special skill might also be struggling to get a job abroad or in a city. If he or she would move to his or her country of origin or to the suburbs with a slightly lower salary, that person might be the next managing director of that company or probably start his/her own business.

The emphasis here is **MOVEMENT**. Obeying the still small voice of God in any challenging moment is very crucial to your survival in any season of change. Remember, God will always direct your footsteps. The steps of a righteous man are ordered by the Lord. There are places where you stay because you have friends nearby. However, if you cannot see the glory of God or His purpose for your life, it will not come to pass. Look at the life of Abraham. God asked him to leave his country, parents and familiar places to the unknown, to receive a promise. At a point in his journey he needed to separate with Lot in order for God to rain on him is abundance. In Isaiah 6:1, Prophet said, 'The day King Uziah died I saw the Lord... Jacob deceived his brother Esau for his blessing'. God asked him to move out else his brother would kill him. All this happened to preserve the coming of the Messiah. Brethren, do not be afraid to be unpopular or to chart the uncharted. God is not a respecter of persons. Look out for those that would deprive you of your anointing or block your opportunities and destroy your favour. One of the things I have realised in ministry or life is that, if God sees you with someone who can even kill you for your blessing, He will delay until that person is eliminated. A typical example can be if you have an accountant who is a thief, God will delay the overflow of cash until that accountant is gone else he will steal all your money.

It is stated in Proverbs 3:5-8, 5 'Trust in the LORD with all your heart and lean not on your own understanding; 6 in all your ways submit to him, and he will make your paths straight. 7 Do not be wise in your own eyes; fear the LORD and shun evil. 8 This will bring health to your body and nourishment to your bones'.

The wisest man who ever lived was King Solomon and his advice is clear in his writings. Acknowledging God in all that we do and obeying His leadings will cause us to survive every change that will occur in our lives and bring massive deliverance.

Warning: Do not stay where you will be tolerated. Go where you will be celebrated. In celebration, do not fool yourself as the praises of men can lead to thinking something right in which the Lord might not be happy. Or sometimes think you are God.

Strategy 4: Method/Tactics/Approach

10 'So he went to Zarephath. When he came to the town gate, a widow was there gathering sticks. He called to her and asked, 'Would you bring me a little water in a jar so I may have a drink?' 11 As she was going to get it, he called, 'And bring me, please, a piece of bread.' 12 'As surely as the LORD your God lives,' she replied, 'I don't have any bread - only a handful of flour in a jar and a little oil in a jug. I am gathering a few sticks to take

home and make a meal for myself and my son, that we may eat it - and die.' 13 Elijah said to her, 'Don't be afraid. Go home and do as you have said. But first make a small cake of bread for me from what you have and bring it to me, and then make something for yourself and your son.' 14 For this is what the LORD, the God of Israel, says: 'The jar of flour will not be used up and the jug of oil will not run dry until the day the LORD gives rain on the land'.

Throughout this change of season in Elijah's life, two things were obvious. One is movement and the second one is his approach, method or tactics in dealing with every situation or place he found himself. He was living in his comfortable house, cooking, eating and drinking by himself. He prophesied and things began to change for him. So his tactics or approach also changed due to change in season or situation.

> ***'You've got to think about big things while you're doing small things, so that all the small things go in the right direction.'***
>
> ***– Alvin Toffler***
>
> 

1. At the brooks, God commanded ravens to feed him and he will just drink from the river. Ravens are animals without will and emotions. So when God sent them, without thinking they will just move.

2. But when he Elijah came to Zarephath, his tactics, method and approach to the whole situation change. When he saw the woman gathering the sticks, he **CALLED** her and **ASKED** and **INSISTED**. Why Elijah would used this approach,

because he is dealing with a human being who has **WILL, EMOTION, FEELINGS** and can **REASON.**

Human beings are such that when God speaks to them, they will still deliberate in their mind, judge to see whether it is from God or their human spirit and more or less they can refuse or resist what God is asking them to do. So Elijah needed to tackle the situation with a different approach, in other words, to gain what he wanted. In an economic downtown or a change in situation, one cannot use the same approach or method of doing business to survive.

Some quotations from Albert Einstein:

'We can't solve problems by using the same kind of thinking we used when we created them.'

'The definition of insanity is doing the same thing over and over again, but expecting different results.'

In this 21st century, Churches, pastors and business executives cannot operate the same way as before the change. New strategies and approaches must be introduced in order to survive the change and thrive. Churches, depending upon their location, must conduct services in such a way that will be fulfilling and meet the needs of the local community. Pastors must be computer literate and update themselves to be able to use these modern facilities to deliver messages in a contemporary way.

The best strategist I have ever known in my life is God's spirit. There are many changes that occurred in the Bible and the main characters always seek God for

His direction in achieving their goal. Examples are: Noah and the flood, Moses and the Israelites' great deliverance, King Jehoshaphat and the battle of his enemies, Joshua and the walls of Jericho; the list goes on.

Dear friend, I might not know what situation or change you are experiencing now, but I can assure you the best person to consult is your Heavenly Father and His spirit will be available in directing you what to do. In James 5, He says in His word, 'If any man lacks wisdom let him ask God who gives to me liberally'. The questions are: are you willing to follow His leadings and directions? Are you willing to put down your will and follow His will? God will not force us to do something we are not willing to do. There are His perfect will and permissive will. A typical example we can find is when Jesus was praying in the Garden of Gethsemane. According to scripture, He prayed earnestly, seeking the Father's perfect will for the cross. In seeking God's perfect will, one thing must stand out and that is **OBEDIENCE.**

Summary

Now that we have looked at the four strategies Elijah adopted through the direction from God in surviving the changes he went through, we can confidently say whatever may come our way we will trust God for His leadings.

I must also say that the above strategies may differ depending upon the situation one is in and the personality involved as we have different callings and purposes to fulfil on Earth. I will encourage everyone to seek the face of God earnestly. Secondly, Godly counselling from proven or experienced men and women of God must be sought, regarding some of these life issues. Having a mentor or a coach can be a good way of steering through life's difficulties instead of being alone.

Thirdly, reading widely has been a good source of acquiring information or knowledge. The Bible says, 'My people perish due to lack of knowledge.

Last but not the least, trust and follow your instincts, inner drive and unleash it. Make sure they are trained properly and in tune with the word of God

CHAPTER 4: OBEDIENCE
(Key to Super-Abundance)
Introduction to Obedience

Have you ever wondered what God's will is for your life? Have you needed to make a difficult decision and wondered what God wanted you to do in that situation?

> ***★ 'You've got to think about big things while you're doing small things, so that all the small things go in the right direction.'***
>
> ***– Alvin Toffler***
>
> ★★★★★★★

We all struggle with questions about our future. Questions like: How can I know God's plan for my life? Which job should I take? Is this the person God wants me to marry? Is this a good investment to make? Should I share the gospel with my boss? You probably have questions you could add to that list.

The greatest discovery I have ever made concerning how to know the will of God involves the following:

- Fully surrendering my life to the Lordship of Christ
- Living a life of obedience in the power of the Holy Spirit
- Maintaining my first love for our Lord

Many Christians are trying so hard to discover the will of God that they lose the joy of the Lord and leave their first love for Him.

But all we need to do is abide in Christ, maintain our first love for Him, and walk in the power of the Holy Spirit; then we will be in the will of God. So as you continue to walk in the Spirit, He will guide you in making the most important decisions of life. He will also guide you in the daily, moment-by-moment decisions and actions of your life.

Speaking of the Holy Spirit, Jesus says, 'When he, the Spirit of truth, comes, he will guide you into all truth... and he will tell you what is yet to come' (John 16:13). So the key to knowing God's will is to be obedient to the guidance of the Holy Spirit of truth. If you are willing to trust and obey God and live a holy life, God will reveal Himself to you and direct your steps as a way of life.

Satan is the enemy of our soul. His mission is to keep us from being effective and fruitful. But although he wields great power, Satan can never defeat us if we are completely yielded and obedient to Christ and His spirit.

Some people are reluctant to trust God completely with their lives, fearing that He may want to make a change in their plans. Yes, He will change our plans. His plans are infinitely better than the very best we could ever conceive.

Is it not logical that the One who created us knows better than us the purpose for which we were created?

And since He loves us enough to die for us, is it not logical to believe that His way is best (Romans 8:32)?

Obedience is the true test or key of our love for Christ and the secret to discovering God's will for our life.

The Widow's Obedience

15 'she went away and did (obey) as Elijah had told her. So there was food every day for Elijah and for the woman and her family'.

I would like us to take a critical look at an in-depth definition of the word obedience from a scriptural point of view, in other words, a holistic view of obedience because 'half obedience is disobedience'. God demands total obedience from us throughout scripture. It also means that you cannot obey God in some aspects of your life and disobey Him in others.

'In the beginning God created the heaven and the Earth.' Genesis 1: 1. Not only did God create the heaven and the Earth, God also, 'created man in his own image, in the image of God created he him, male and female created he them'. Genesis 1:27.

Every member of the whole human race is loved mightily and tenderly by God our Creator. Whatever God has ever done for the human race, he has done out of genuine love, and with an intense desire to see man happy. In the Book, the Bible, our loving heavenly Father and beneficent Creator has revealed unto the human race His divine will.

Everything God has ever said to us in His Holy Book has been said for our own good, and is conducive to our happiness here in this life, and in the life that is to come. Our obedience, therefore to God's only will as revealed in the Bible, is for our own personal happiness and eternal welfare.

> ★ ***'Perpetual optimism is a force multiplier.'***
>
> ***– Colin Powell***
>
> 

A study of the Bible and of human history reveals that man's obedience to God's will has always brought happiness, and disobedience has always brought unhappiness. For this reason we have in the Bible an emphasis on obedience. God said, 'The things I command you, observe to do'. **Deuteronomy 12:32**. Again, 'If you be willing and obedient, you shall eat the good of the land.' **Isaiah 1:19**.

Christ himself set the example of obedience to the Father's will. 'Though he was a Son, yet learned he obedience by the things which he suffered; and being made perfect, he became the author of eternal salvation unto all them that obey him'. **Hebrews 5:8,9**. Christ said, 'I came down from heaven, not to do mine own **will**, but the will of him that sent me' **John 6: 38**. Again Christ said, 'Not everyone that saith unto me, Lord, Lord, shall enter into the kingdom of heaven; but he that doeth the will of my father which is in heaven' **Matthew 7:21**. The inspired Apostle John said, 'He that doeth the will of God abideth forever' **I John 2:17.**

Man must come to know God and his Son, Jesus Christ. Jesus said, 'This is life eternal, that they might know thee the only true God, and Jesus Christ whom thou has sent' **John 17:3.** Eternal life thus depends on our knowing God. But how do we know that we know God? 'Hereby we know that we know him, if we keep his commandments' I John 2:3. We cannot claim scripturally to know God, if we refuse to keep his commandments. Obedience shows we know God.

Man needs friendship with God and his Son. Jesus said, 'Ye are my friends, if you do whatsoever I command you' John 15:14.

Obedience is an expression of our friendship with Jesus. What a marvellous friend we have in him! Every human being needs this close friendship with our blessed Lord. Obedience shows our friendship. Faith in Jesus Christ as God's Son is essential to our salvation from sin.

'Believe on the Lord Jesus Christ, and thou shalt be saved' [Acts 16:31].

But our faith is not a saving faith unless it expresses itself in obedience to God's will. The inspired James said, 'For as the body without the spirit is dead, so faith without works is dead also.

'James 2:26. Saving faith expresses itself in obedience to God's will.

Certainly we know that love for God on our part is indispensable. But love expresses itself in obedience. 'If you love me, keep my commandments', said Jesus in John 14:15.

Vocal claims of love for God and His Son are empty sounds unless they come from the hearts of faith, finding expression in willing, loving obedience to God's will. Faithful obedience to God shows we love God.

In the Old Testament the Hebrew word *shama* means 'to hear, listen, obey'.

Exodus writes in full for all.

Exodus 19:5 - 'if you obey My voice... you shall be My possession'.

Exod. 24:7 - 'All that the Lord has spoken we will do; we will be obedient'.

Deut. 11:13 - 'if you listen obediently to My commandments'.

I Sam. 15:22 -'to obey is better than sacrifice'.

In the New Testament is the Greek word *hupakouo*means 'to listen under, to obey'; the opposite is *parakouo*- 'to listen around, beside, disobedience'.

Rom. 16:26 - 'obedience of faith'.

II Cor. 10:5 -'taking every thought captive to the obedience of Christ'.

II Thess. 1:8 - 'those who do not obey the gospel of our Lord Jesus'.

I Pet. 1:2 - 'that you may obey Jesus Christ'.

I Pet. 1:14 - 'As obedient children...be holy'.

I Pet. 1:22 - 'you have in obedience to the truth purified your souls'.

However, the Greek words *peitho* and *peitharcheo* mean 'to persuade, convince'. The opposite is *apeitheo* which means to be 'unconvinced, disobedient'.

Acts 5:29 - 'we must obey God rather than men'.

Acts 5:32 - 'the Spirit whom God has given to those who obey Him.

Obedience can be defined as

Etymology - Latin *oboedire- ob=* towards; *oedire=* 'to hear'.

In popular English usage it means: 'to follow, heed, and comply with commands or injunctions within a sphere of jurisdiction. We can also say, 'Obedience pertains to listening to (and responding to) God, Moses, prophets, Jesus, Paul, parents, etc'. Obedience has also been developed as a law-based interpretation:

(1) rule-keeping
(2) commandment compliance
(3) performance according to precepts

In 2 Chronicles 20:20, it is stated: 'Believe in the Lord your God, so shall ye be established; believe his prophets, so shall ye prosper'.

This is exactly what the widow did. She believed the words of the Prophet Elijah and by so doing she ended up reaping super-abundance during a dry or lean season. Whose voice are you hearing and obeying? Remember, many are the voices in this world but none of them are without significance. A word from a man or your spiritual father (Pastor) can bring a tremendous change in your life, family and business. Elijah moved into the widow's life by divine direction. Sometimes, a man of God might visit your church or during special church programmes such as conferences or revival meetings and a word might come out to sow a seed into the man of God's life. This act of faith can release supernatural provision because some men of God carry special grace of God's provision. **I can boldly say I am one of them.** I have many testimonies from people who sowed into my life or ministry and God supernaturally rewarded them or preached in churches and raised funds and those who gave reaped tremendously and were blessed in a variety of areas such as a new job, new contract, status regularisation, marriage, health etc.

★ ***'The man of thought who will not act is ineffective; the man of action who will not think is dangerous.'***

– Richard M. Nixon

Warning! Do not move because you want to move or the man is an articulate speaker but rather move because God is asking you to move. Be sensitive to the voice of the Holy Spirit i.e. the inner witness.

CHAPTER 5
Bouncing Back Strongly

You can blame people or circumstances for pushing you down but you cannot continue to blame them for lying down there. Life will always throw you storms and challenges of life but your reaction to them will determine how you survive or bounce back. When life hits or knocks you hard, try to fall on your back and if you can look up, you can always rise up.

Attitude is everything. Attitude has always been a determining factor in the way we see things and our reaction to things. Whether you will succeed in life or not is, on the whole, determined by your attitude towards life. Something you may see as opposition might be someone else's opportunity. Take the example of a storm. You will normally see many people running away whenever the Met Office forecasts there is going to be a storm. At the same time you see few people running towards the storm. The difference is that the majority sees the storm as an opposition whilst the few sees it as an opportunity to take pictures or report it in the media to make news and by so doing they make money. All has got to do with

> ***'Success is not final, failure is not fatal: it is the courage to continue that counts.'***
>
> ***– Winston S. Churchill***
>
> ★★★★★★★

your perception and attitude. How do you view life? What self-portrait do you carry about yourself? Are you living your life based on people's opinion about you or what God says? Both Elijah the man of God and the widow and her family according the passage ate in plenty until the rain came back according to the man of God's words.

16. 'For the jar of flour was not used up and the jug of oil did not run dry, in keeping with the word of the Lord spoken by Elijah'.

The Coming Wealth Transfer

But the wealth of the sinner is stored up for the righteous. Proverbs 13:22.

In the last days there will be a transfer of wealth into the hands of the believers or righteous as the Bible puts it for the purpose of funding a great commission of souls and for believers have greater influence on society in the name of Jesus Christ. There are many ways I believe God will be bringing it. In the case of the widow, it was her obedience to the prophet's instruction and more importantly what she had in her house (flour and oil). God can only use what you have in your hands or house.

For the purpose of this work, I will limit myself to four ways I strongly believe in my spirit as I write this book God is going to use in bringing this great wealth to believers.

1. **Supernatural transfer**: - God lives in the supernatural and only He can do what is beyond the

natural. God gave the Israelites favour in the sight of the Egyptians. The Egyptians gave them wahtever the Israelites asked when they were leaving Egypt for the Promised Land. I believe genuine Christian organisations and not-for-profit Christian organisations will receive major gifts and donations from individuals or foundations to carry out their Christian missions.

2. **Power to Make Wealth**: - God is going to give witty ideas and inventions to believers throughout the world that will generate wealth. This has already began I believe there are more Christian businessmen and women than we used to know.

3. **Social Entrepreneurship**: - Just as Joseph was entrusted with the resources of Egypt to solve a societal problem resulting from a famine in the land, God is good to transfer money to believers who are solving societal problems. Governments will fund private enterprises because government has not been able to do it all.

4. **Wealthy Individuals Conversion**: - Finally, many non-believers who are wealthy will become Christians in these last days and will begin to use their wealth for Kingdom purposes.

Deuteronomy 8:18 ***'But remember the Lord your God, for it is He who gives you the ability to produce wealth, and so confirms His covenant, which He swore to your fathers, as it is today.***

We must remember according to scripture, the coming wealth transfer is not only for our personal agendas and goals but rather for Kingdom expansion.

By the act of faith in the man of God, divine inspiration and miracle power of Jehovah-jireh, the jar of flour was not used up and the jug of oil did not run dry. What a divine provision for this widow and her son. Hearing God's still-small voice in the midst of a famine will always cause a tremendous breakthrough.

I might not know who you are but hear me very carefully. There is abundance coming in these last days but it will only be for those who are willing and ready to give it up for the Kingdom of God and its expansion.

You have been down but you are coming up and remember, above all, that God is your helper. Strong faith in God and His word will definitely cause you to bounce back strongly.

In the case of the widow, she and her son bounced back strongly after the lean season. That is what our God can do.

Ephesians 3:20, 'Unto Him who is able to do more, exceedingly abundantly, above all that we can think of or imagine according to the power which is at work in us'.

I prophesy under the inspiration of the almighty God, whoever is reading this book: if there is a change or a lean season you are going through, whether physical or spiritual, financial, marital or any kind of change and it seems as if you are getting to the end of the road of your life: may God who sent the man of God into the widow's life, send a deliverer into your life now. Amen. And if you have it or have God's spirit upon your life, May God send you as an Elijah into someone else's life who needs help.

I declare and decree into your life, family, business and community that the Lord answers you in the day of trouble, famine and scarcity.

May the name of the God of Jacob defend you.

May He send you help from the sanctuary, and strengthen you out of your place of dwelling;May He remember all your offerings and tithes, accept your burnt offerings;

May He grant you according to your heart's desire and fulfil all your purpose and answer you from His Holy dwellings of the third Heavens.

I bless you in the name of our Lord Jesus Christ the soon-coming King.

If you have been blessed by the timeless principles of His word and this book, do get in touch and let us hear your testimonies. Amen.

Shalom, life and peace to you all, my good friends.

NOTE

Firstly, making this work relevant to today's reader most of the scriptures were taken from the New King James Bible (NKJV) and other translations as well.

Secondly, the internet was widely used to further explain text and subject matters.

REFERENCES

http://www.theoryofchange.org/what-is-theory-of-change/

http://searchcio.techtarget.com/definition/change-management

http://smallbusiness.chron.com/change-important-organization-728.html

Albrecht, K. 1980. *Brain Power: Learning to Improve Your Thinking Skills*. New York: Simon and Schuster.

Allaire, Y., and M. E. Firsirotu, M.E. 1984. Theories of organizational culture. *Organization Studies* 5:193-226.

Allen, R.W., et al. 1979. Organizational politics: Tactics and characteristics of its actors. *California Management Review* 22: 77-83.

Andrews, Kenneth. 1989. Ethics in practice. *Harvard Business Review* (Sept- Oct): 99-104.

Argyris, Chris. 1987. Double loop learning in organizations. *Harvard Business Review* (Sept-Oct): 115-125.

Ashforth, B.E., and F. Mael. Social identity theory and the organization. *Academy of Management Review* 14 (1): 20-39.

Ashmos, D.P., and G.P Huber. 1987 The systems paradigm in organizational theory: Correcting the record and suggesting the future. *Academy of Management Review* 12 (4): 607-621.

Augustine, Norman R. 1987. Reshaping an industry: lockheed martin's survival story. *Harvard Business Review* (May-June).

Barasch, Douglas, S. 1987. God and toothpaste. New York Times Magazine.

Barrick, M. R., and M.K. Mount. 1991. The big five personality dimensions and job performance: a meta-analysis. *Personnel Psychology* 44: 1-26.

Bass, B. M. 1985. *Leadership and performance beyond expectation*. New York: Free Press.

Becker, H.S., and B. Geer. Latent culture. *Administrative Science Quarterly* 5: 303-313.

Bedke,Curtis M. 1993. Strategic decisionmaking in a multinational ad hoc coalition ad astra per aspera. Unpublished ICAF course paper, 17 December: 9.

Bennis, Warren. 1989. *On Becoming a Leader*. Reading, MA: Addison-Wesley Publishing Co., Inc.

Wilgoren, Debbi, *The Washington Post*, March 28, Al9.

Willbern, York. 1984. Types and Levels of public morality. *Public Administration Review* (March-April): 102-108.

Wuthnow, R., and M. Witten, M. 1988. New directions in the study of culture. *Annual Review of Sociology* 14: 50-51

Yates, Douyglas Jr. 1987. *The Politics of Management* .San Francisco: Jossey-Bass Publishers.

Yukl, G. 1994. *Leadership in Organizations*. Englewood Cliffs, NJ: Prentice Hall.

Zaccaro, S. J. 1996. *Models and Theories of Executive Leadership: A Conceptual/Empirical Review and Integration*. Alexandria, VA: U.S. Army Research Institute for the Behavioral and Social Sciences.

Zald, M.N., and M.A. Berger. Social movements in organizations. *American Journal of Sociology* 83 (4): 240-259.

Zsambok, Caroline E., Gary Klein,, Molly M. Kyne, and David W. Klinger. 1992. *Advanced Team Decision Making: A Developmental Model.* Fairborn, OH: Klein Associates Inc.

ND - #0265 - 080726 - C0 - 197/132/7 - PB - 9781784562687 - Gloss Lamination